Joke Books

Jokes about Bugs

by Judy A. Winter

Consulting Editor: Gail Saunders-Smith, PhD

CAPSTONE PRESS
a capstone imprint

Pebble Books are published by Capstone Press,
151 Good Counsel Drive, P.O. Box 669, Mankato, Minnesota 56002.
www.capstonepub.com

Library of Congress Cataloging-in-Publication Data
Winter, Judy A., 1952–
  Jokes about bugs / by Judy A. Winter.
    p. cm.—(Pebble books. Joke books)
  Includes bibliographical references.
  Summary: "Simple text and photographs present jokes about bugs"—Provided by
publisher.
  ISBN 978-1-4296-4997-1 (library binding)
  1. Insects—Juvenile humor. I. Title. II. Series.
  PN6231.I56W56 2011
  818'.602—dc22   2010002323

Editorial Credits
Gillia Olson, editor; Ted Williams, designer; Sarah Schuette, studio specialist;
    Marcy Morin, studio scheduler; Eric Manske, production specialist

Photo Credits
All photos by Capstone Studio: Karon Dubke except: BigStockPhoto.com: hudakore,
10 (fireflies); Shutterstock: Apollofoto, 12 (shoes), Audrey Snider-Bell, 12 (centipede),
Christian Kieffer, 14 (car), Eric Isselée, 4 (ladybug), Jan Quist, cover, 18 (dung beetle),
Joseph Calev, 6 (bee), PaulPaladin, 22 (grass), Pinchuk Alexey, 10 (race track),
RTimages, 14 (steering wheel), South 12th Photography, 14 (spider), trucic, background
(throughout), Valentyn Kolesnyk (ValeKo), 16 (cockroach)

Note to Parents and Teachers

The Joke Books set supports English language arts standards related
to reading a wide range of print for personal fulfillment. Early readers
may need assistance to read some of the words and to use the Table of
Contents, Read More, and Internet Sites sections of this book.

Table of Contents

What did the bug say after it hit the window?

If I had the guts, I would do it again.

What bug can't go into the mens' bathroom?

A ladybug.

What goes zzub, zzub?
A bee flying backward.

What do bees chew?
Bumble gum.

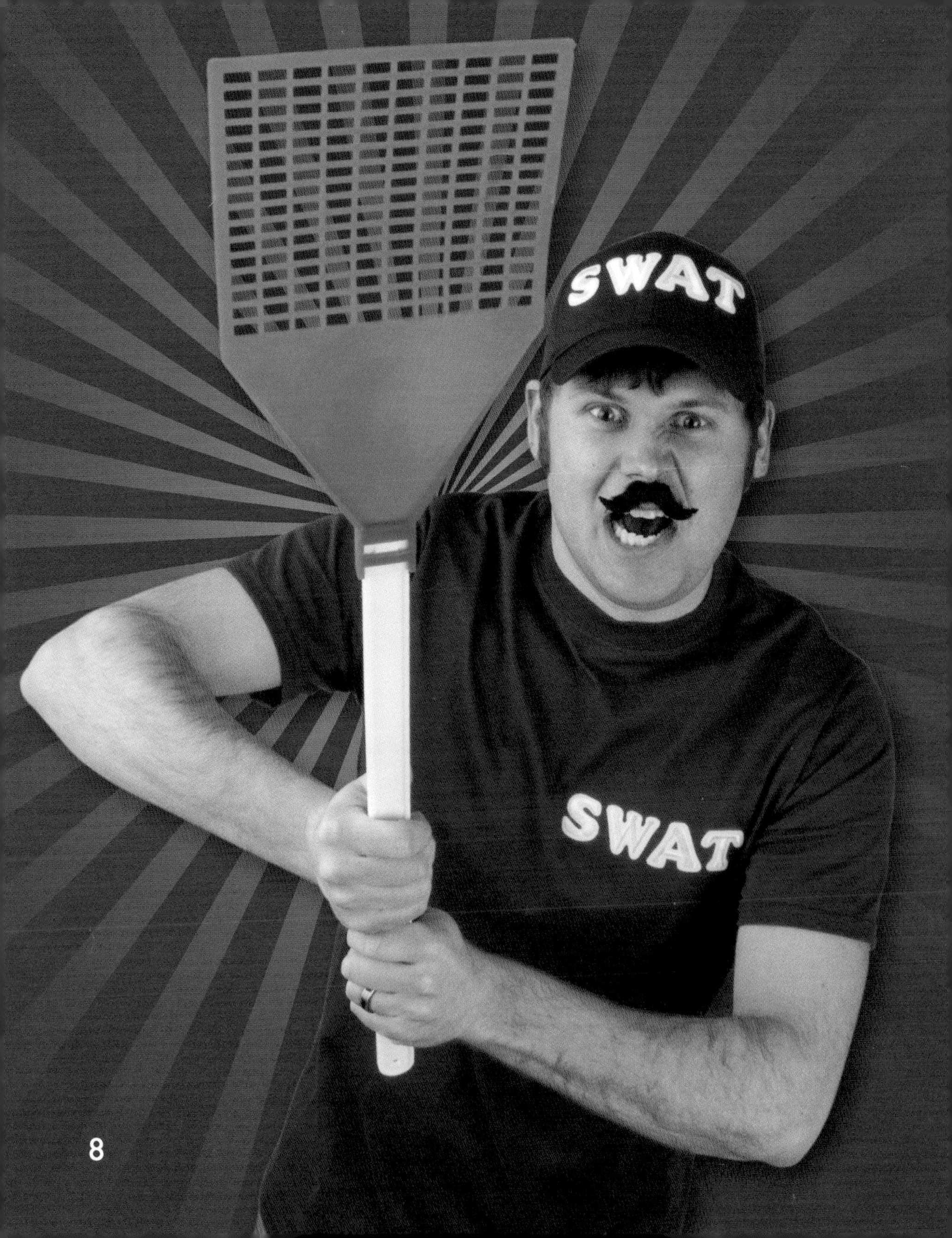
SWAT
SWAT

How did the police get rid of the flies?

They called in the SWAT team.

What do you call a fly with no wings?

A walk.

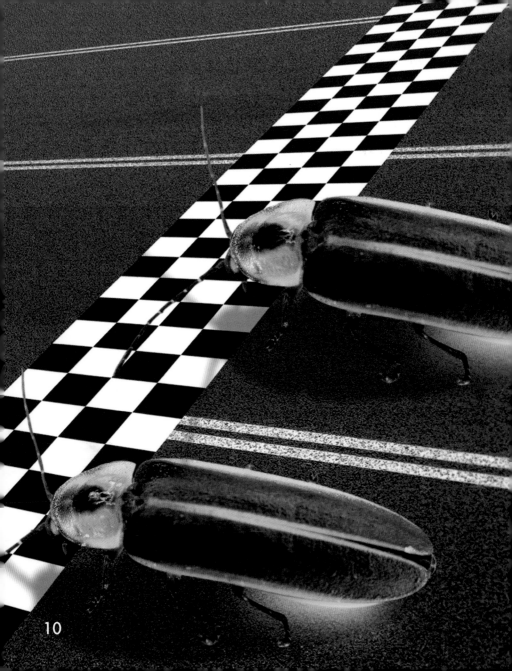

How do fireflies
start a race?

**On your mark,
get set, glow!**

Why was the mom
firefly sad?

**Her kids weren't
that bright.**

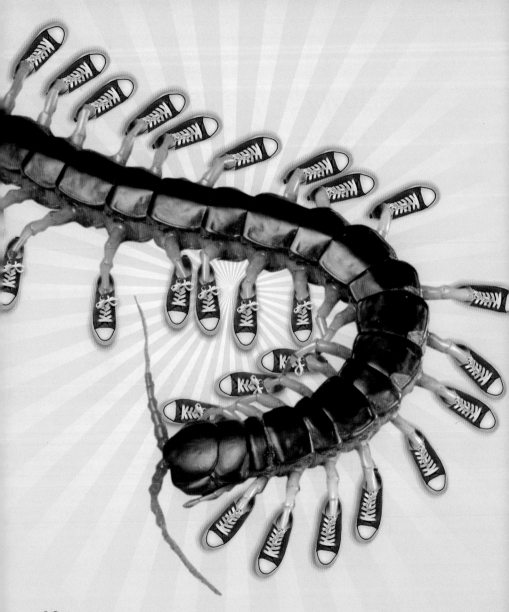

What is worse than a giraffe with a sore throat?

A centipede with sore feet.

What do centipedes spend all their money on?

New shoes.

What did the spider do when he bought a new car?

He took it out for a spin.

What do you call two spiders that just got married?

Newlywebs.

How many cockroaches does it take to screw in a light bulb?

No one knows. When the light comes on, they scatter.

Have you seen a kicking cockroach? **It's the nasty bug that's going around.**

What did the dung
beetle say to the toilet?
You look a little flushed.

Why did the dung beetle
take toilet paper to the party?
**Because he was a
party pooper.**

Why did the girl throw butter out the window?

She wanted to see the butter-fly.

What do you get when you eat caterpillars?

Butterflies in your stomach.

Why was the caterpillar thrown out of the park?

He turned into a litter bug.

What did the caterpillar say to the leaf?

It's been nice gnawing you.

Read More

Horsfall, Jacqueline. *Bug Jokes.* Giggle Fit.
New York: Sterling, 2006.

Moore, Mark. *Creepy Crawlers: A Book of Bug Jokes.*
Read It! Joke Books. Minneapolis: Picture Window
Books, 2005.

Rosenberg, Pam. *Bug Jokes.* Laughing Matters.
Chanhassen, Minn.: Child's World, 2007.

Internet Sites

FactHound offers a safe, fun way to find Internet sites
related to this book. All of the sites on FactHound have
been researched by our staff.

Here's all you do:

Visit *www.facthound.com*

Type in this code: 9781429649971

Word Count: 268 **Grade:** 1
Early-Intervention Level: 18